COMMON UPROAR

COMMON UPROAR

Michael Bowden

Concrete Wolf
Louis Award Series

Copyright © 2020 Michael Bowden

All rights reserved. No part of this publication may be reproduced, distributed, or transmitted in any form or by any means whatsoever, without written permission from the publisher, except in the case of brief excerpts for critical reviews and articles.
All inquiries should be addressed to Concrete Wolf Press.

Concrete Wolf
Louis Award Series

Poetry
ISBN 978-0-578-59344-9

Design: Tonya Namura using Cochin

Cover photo by Tony Aragon

Author photos by Pauline Fredericks

Concrete Wolf
PO Box 445
Tillamook, OR 97141

http://ConcreteWolf.com

ConcreteWolfPress@gmail.com

for Chacha

ACKNOWLEDGMENTS

My gratitude to the editors of the following publications in which many of these poems first appeared, some of them in slightly different versions.

Birmingham Poetry Review: "December Fires" and "The Labor of Blossoms" (entitled "Linkage")

Bluff City: "The Same River Twice"

Carolina Quarterly: "Miller Canyon Trail No. 106"

Chariton Review: "The Diary of Crows"

Cloudbank: "Big World, Little Garden" and "Ellipsis in Memory of Lorca and Love"

Crazyhorse: "Returning from Fields, Thinking of My Father"

Graham House Review: "Watering the Mare"

Greenfield Review: "Freight"

Hayden's Ferry Review: "Hunter's Moon" and "Of the Small"

Hiram Poetry Review: "Elegy for a Broken Kite" (entitled "Keeper")

Illuminations: "Greenland"

Louisville Review: "Little Colorado"

Mid-American Review: "Flying Cloud"

Passages North: "Redtail Hawks"

Poetry East: "Improvisation on a Trail Sign Phrase" and "Plenty"

The Prose Poem: An International Journal: "Yellow Weeds"

Seattle Review: "Relocating"

Sonora Review: "Lowell Observatory" and "Petition"

Southern Poetry Review: "Resolution"

Sow's Ear Poetry Review: "Patterns" and "Sonoita Races"

Tucson Guide Quarterly: "Sonora"

Verse: "Locomotives"

West Branch: "Garcia's Hand"

Willow Springs Magazine: "Winter Count"

Yarrow: "Clare"

"Song" was originally published in *The Party Train: A Collection of North American Prose Poetry* (New Rivers Press, 1996).

"Miller Canyon Trail No. 106" was anthologized in *The Pushcart Prize XV* (Pushcart Press, 1990).

My thanks to the Arizona Commission on the Arts for a pair of Creative Writing Fellowships in Poetry, during which many of these poems were written.

CONTENTS

Acknowledgments — vii

PART I: THE VANISHED TEXTS
Improvisation on a Trail Sign Phrase — 5
Returning from Fields, Thinking of My Father — 6
Flying Cloud — 8
Locomotives — 10
Greenland — 11
Clare — 12
Elegy for a Broken Kite — 14
Improvisation on a Fragment from
 Miguel Hernandez — 15
Resolution — 16
Mystical Ballast — 17
Little Colorado — 18
Both — 20
Ellipsis in Memory of Lorca and Love — 21
Petition — 22

PART II: THE LABOR OF BLOSSOMS
Winter Count — 27
The Diary of Crows — 29
Lowell Observatory — 30
Watering the Mare — 32
Garcia's Hand — 33
Sonoita Races — 34
The Labor of Blossoms — 35
Song — 37
Hunter's Moon — 38
The Same River Twice — 39
Let Us, Like Issa, Ask Ourselves — 41
Absence — 42

Redtail Hawks	43
Of the Small	44
Big World, Little Garden	45
Miller Canyon Trail No. 106	48

PART III: HERE A MOMENT

Whitewater Draw	53
After the Flood	54
Handmade to Last	55
Freight	57
First Spring, Summer Tanager	58
Sonora	60
Relocating	62
Dawn Comes to a Small Farm in Southeast Arizona	64
Yellow Weeds	65
Old Sawmill Spring	66
December Fires	67
Plenty	69
Patterns	70
Gratitude	73
About the Author	75

COMMON UPROAR

PART I

THE VANISHED TEXTS

Would I love it this way if it could last
—W.S. Merwin

Improvisation on a Trail Sign Phrase

in dry seasons the stream is ephemeral

dusty toe shoe on the up-canyon path

a fawn's cracked hoof dragged from its bier

first a man's grave then the ruin of the house

memory time's broken playlist

an old woman stitching, losing her sight

evenings father read to mother at the forest's edge

a butterfly fanning its wings

lost mountain spring, lost cup of hands

the lines all meet somewhere beyond this ridge

in April each morning the light more direct

Returning from Fields, Thinking of My Father

Listen to them low.
Listen long enough and their voices travel a spectrum
from absurd to profound,
though no one's flattered
tightening fence against stock.

The pasture's overgrazed and the bastards want in —
that's all.

So what do we make of a lone crow soaring into leaves,
a mystery of limbs
beyond the field,
and how what once passed for a kind of holy land
diminishes? Geriatric, the world
repeats itself.

My father's veins thread through my arms,
coarse as blue twine.
When I look at them I think of him
home from the shop's
six chairs — *no waiting* —
and its infinite regression of mirrors.

Weekends he counts the take over and over,
brush paints a thin tree
on the living room wall.
It grows slowly,
like a family,
like a till's stack of notes ledgered each Sunday.

But now as I return
from fields and wrens nervous and burying
their faces in their chests —

now as I pass unnoticed —
I want to deny everything they sing can be translated
appetite.

I want to look hard at what I've ignored.
I want to begin with the artless sky.

Flying Cloud

A boy at table, fork in hand,
I called green beans
birds on a line.
Somehow in 1959
that made them easier to swallow,
though no ad-libbed rite
after supper
moved my dad any faster
when he finally began the instructions.

Intense with care
as mom scouting shoots in spring,
he took an inventory of parts,
then filed the hull,
the masts, the whole ordered complexity
of sails with emery board
until I couldn't keep my feet still,
and begged and whined
to the silence for glue.

He knew we had time.
Leisurely, with a fine camel-hair
laid on paint
from the kit's jaunty bottles:
red wheelhouse roof,
blue lifeboats—
turquoise mermaid he called the ship's eyes.

I was content, watching her dry,
gently inhaling the Testors—
in my mind already steering
for a white island
under the Christmas tree.
He had climbed into his next miracle,

a slack of lights
wound through his arm like ready stars—
a sort of bell's tongue
hammering the eaves until our house stood trimmed.

While over his shoulder you could see
constellations,
in winter that hunter
who always seemed more lonely
than brave.
You could understand patience
when wind stroked my father's hair,
its dark sheen of cats.
You could feel
Colossus breathing in the skinny mulberries.

Locomotives
after Leon-Paul Fargue

Peach fuzz on her chin she plucked with a mirror and tweezers. A fringe of strawberries hanging from the hem of the curtains. A rolling pin for thinning dough. A wooden cane redeemed with Green Stamps for walking. And the black Bible on a bookshelf. Open the cover. You'll find her name written there. In the bowl, a slice of white bread, sprinkled with sugar. Covered with milk. The orange cat sitting patiently, washing his face. Not far from the back door, a street of potholes leading to the railroad crossing where tracks lie blue in early light. Empty. If you follow the cat past the small rhubarb garden, you can stand in the shifting gray cinders there and wonder where the great locomotives have gone, trailing their coaches in the cold. Leaving their phrases of steam in that place where unscrubbed brats eat their own snots. Where you were warned not to play. The boogers will eat holes in their stomachs, she scolded. Oh, let him be, the man with the whiskers said. Meanwhile, on the old, dark table, a tin of throat lozenges, each wrapped in foil. The bottle of cherry cough syrup. A yellow moon of cardboard hidden under its black cap where you secretly ran your tongue. It tasted of melancholy but it will be years before you have a word for that—when you're old enough to know the time without consulting a watch, and a poem in a book by a man long dead still has the power to take you back into the strange and exquisite arms of memories. Those masters of childhood, vigilant at their desks. Forever calling on each of us, in turn.

Greenland

The heaviness of time is what we hear when we listen to rain drumming the roof. All day it has fallen, and in the distant mountains it has jacketed the peaks with snow. Yesterday sweet clouds of rhubarb boiled off the range, filling the house. In the backyard a boy and his grandfather peering into the ashes of a freezer box. A transformation leaving one of them with a judicial expression. Time just beginning to take things away. For the rest of his life he'll grow lighter. Soon the immaculate gray *Bel Air* will back from the garage. Hose uncoiled, the old man directs water along the concrete floor beneath a pinned world of fading nations: *Belgian Congo, Siam*. The fat orange cat meditating on the workbench reminds the boy of a Buddha smiling from the pages of a book he found inside. When the whiskered man hands him the broom he notices how large his old eyes have grown behind their lenses. How close to his scalp the cut of his bristly hair. For the first time he's aware of this architecture of revision, this future of disjointed pasts now under construction in memory. It's the house made of water slipping through our hands. The place we call *home*—that looming island in Mercator's exaggerated projection: Greenland, torn and curling into the vast blue dust of the North Atlantic.

Clare

Sparse clouds and a faint moon —
Where can the bridge be built?
        — Hsu Tsuan-Tseng

Outside the horizon shimmers
on the edge of darkness.
That is why I think of Clare

as a straw-haired girl
come home from the foundry with Daddy whistling on
a watermelon wagon:

She's the last of her generation
in our family.

Now that the sun's down the Siamese enters
and declares
the essential mystery of himself,
circles into sleep
with the authority of a syllogism.

Can this devourer of birds
be Buddha too?

Must Clare,
like all the others,
be remembered in a handful of insufficient gestures —
spinning child racing the dog to Mother, rural teacher
staring after shoes down a well?

What can I make, after all,
of an ordinary pond
in autumn
and a blue void of sky —

A bridge of magpies—

And who can stand on that?

Elegy for a Broken Kite

Someone's been x-ing the days on a calendar. Someone's been sipping tea from a plastic cup on the nightstand. And the sterilized straw, the unopened butter crackers in transparent wrappers next to the ruin of a garden salad, aren't talking. There will be no renewal for the lone petal fallen from its vase onto the linen tablecloth. For its thorned stem in the water which already sours. No song will issue from the darkness in the throat of a bird pulled from the pool's skimmer by maintenance this morning. After the changing of the sheets and the balancing of accounts there will be no resurrection. Because no one knows what to say they'll say she lost her senses. She rose in the middle of the night, she went down, she went out of this world shouting and cursing the orderly. Her body shrunken. Little more than a soul clothed in sharp bone and translucent blue skin. A broken kite made of stick and tissue paper. Though it makes no difference, you have to admire that toughness in the end. That desperation at the expense of grace. Her last words, their beautiful profanity: *Let me go you son of a bitch.*

Improvisation on a Fragment from Miguel Hernandez

a sad goldfish bowl,
a pen of dying nightingales.

Hobbled in a field of wolves, my heart is waiting
on a person of interest who never shows. Words

keep their distance, half-afraid of what I might say,
their legendary heft all lip-service, bluster, and bluff.

A timid sun drags itself from bed over the strip mall.
A scabbed coyote with an agate overcoat runs vacant

asphalt near the Office Max sign asking if I want
to join their team. For a moment, the world is normal,

and then there's nothing normal in the world again.
The morning breeze whispers to a garden gnome,

a gray bird pauses in a gray branch, bobbing over silence
in a winter lawn, wondering where to go from here.

Light intensifies. Isn't that what light's supposed to do?
I can't understand any of it, this tale of nitro tablets

and fear. Sorrow's startled blue thrushes that won't sing,
caged in sockets where your eyes should be as Mother's

hand crosses the yellow resort chair, smoothing your
wings, and I fish this snowfall of the unlikely alone.

Resolution

I'm scraping my father's tool shed,
sanding the surface for two new coats
of Dunn Edwards. One of these days

I'll get inside and rearrange the pegboard
stanzas of pliers and wrenches,
sacks of bone meal, gypsum, and seed,

brush webs from *Everyday Plumbing*
and *Practical Electricity*—what he read
to teach himself what he didn't know.

Tired of stooping with his wire brush,
I stretch, my hands on my hips.
One day, I'll sort what's worth keeping.

Mystical Ballast

fall gusts through mountain aspen

a billion prayer flags

turning on stems against themselves

rain clatter where there is no rain

a minor key

in the quiet language of the grove

the self's erosion stepping through gray thorn

a field unmasking the motionless doe

wild mint, a jay's blue feather

mystical ballast

in your shirt pocket

trees yellow clouds

coming apart where the black trail goes

Little Colorado

Most of the time you don't see them.
You feel them,
if you're careful
not to let your shadow cross the stream.

You feel them moving under surfaces
of cloud and pine,
steady among the great fallen
stones, the slabs tilted into water
like markers in graveyard ruins.

You feel them strike and take your line,
letting them run with the worm
in the frowning mouth,
giving the mouth time—

then, tip up, reeling,
pulling firmly against firm pulling,
you're twins vectoring opposite directions
from the fulcrum of a mirror
thick with winged insects,
as if shards of unraveled fabric

were about to coalesce into some lost
god in forest exile
at the precise moment
you lift him free of the pool,

and the violent drowning begins in birdsong,
in the warm radiance of dawn
overrunning this river of serious mystery.

Now, as your rank hands work
to reclaim the hook
from the night crawler
wound like coiled guts in the throat,
consciousness shears
inside you, standing apart to watch

your eye looking into the eye of the trout,
your eye looking back, reflected
over gills slashing open
the green and yellow flanks of beauty,

until you're no longer certain
if you're the watcher,
or the watched,
in this wood of tangled lines
where tackle snagged,
or bait was cut, and something got away.

Both

The place we chose
looked out across the border
where he hunted.

The going steep, you carried
the owl in rolled canvas.
I shouldered a spade.

Digging, we spelled each other,
folded wings slowly,
laid him in the earth's mouth.

Green eyes, a sharp yellow beak,
the last we saw of him.
Leaned, then, into hillside,

passed a pint in silence,
connected to the world,
separate from it.

Ellipsis in Memory of Lorca and Love
I want to sleep the dream of the apples…
—Federico Garcia Lorca

Three deer look up from their reflections.
They too have been considering
the depth of wooded shadows,

the silence underlying the song of waters,
the strangeness of their motionless bodies
beneath clouds passing through the sky.

They too are feeling the wind take hold of them,
the seconds becoming Ages
while they bend to drink broken sunlight

from the river as it flows away.
All the vanished texts survive:
green apples, cheese, a goatskin of sangria—

the voice reading the words of the Spanish poets
in exile, imprisoned, stood against a wall and shot,
the bullet holes in stucco a repeating ellipsis.

An unmarked grave, we are young and single.
We will become what is missing,
it says here on the stone

in the stream where the swallowtail opens
the yellowed quarto of her wings,
and the dark faces of deer lift from water.

Petition

Give us this day
a gate by the pond
no one uses anymore.
Cottonwood
elegant in winter
as statuary.

Wrens that stir
in pomegranates.
Give us
our share
of the quotidian
miracle —

not innocence,
nor denial,
but admiration
for the one red bird
that blazes
a moment in brush
like a metaphysics.

Allow us once more
the conspiracy
of self and twig,
of leaves
flooring the wood
in parchment —
these vocal
patches of color
issuing language,
thrushes and wrens.

Let us enjoy again
the lively dance
of that ordinary fellow,
leaf-gray himself,

who conceals
dawn under wings
lifted, who kicks
dead growth away
and protests,
his voice small
until it joins
the common uproar.

PART II

THE LABOR OF BLOSSOMS

One anchorage of sand appears as another dissolves away.
—Po Chu-i

Winter Count

In flaked gold rims
each lens reflects a window
filling with clouds,
a tree. It is the tree

whose sharp and numerous branches
fix stars in place at night,
sifting them through sleep,
allowing me this vision
this morning
of the straw grail

balanced in wind. Birds untangle
from the sky,
build here
because cold rain approaches
the western slope of the Sierra,
and snow falls
over Utah and Colorado.

In Salt Lake my sister holds too,
her first son to his first winter,
his mouth at the window hard
and round learning to say
cold, cold. Leaving the house

for the butte, I hear how gray sky
means in horses coming
like hearth fire igniting
the tough heartwood of mesquite,

conjures a myth or a memory:
under moonlight
my back to the bluff,

my eyes fastened on blue ponies
away in the field,

mouth slashing in the cold
to say love
I am cold. Come near.

The Diary of Crows

*That quick, her train caught up over her arm
she ran out of the mirror like a cloud.*
   —William Faulkner

Their wings turn slow. Their wings are almost graceful
turning sharp sky over the motionless reservoir.
They know such uncomplicated movement as we know

names and places in our memories. Like her recollection
of brother and sister stalking birds in North Dakota,
fall knotted in a rainbow of leaves and branches

at their backs. In the *Diary of Crows* nothing
and everything changes. I'm still the old best man,
or a touch of her solitary brother. She has my

blonde sister's eyes. She's no longer a bride,
but a wife, an ampersand of shadow leaning near
the river, like a poet over her journal in marginal

Baltic light. She wears a necklace of crows.
They circle her reflection and enter my mouth
in saying this. Something makes us afraid.

Maybe it's the autumn deer breaking from reeds
like a mandala exploding, spooked by our
unexpected horses. Perhaps the season. Cold blood

thickens, moves slow, a tired watch winding down.
She smiles and her unhinged hair scrapes the sky. I find
myself contemplating my lost sister's porcelain complexion.

                              for Patty

Lowell Observatory

The study of the heavens
requires that the human body become abstract.
        —Percival Lowell

Nine years have passed since I last climbed
this hill. Love, that seems a miracle
no less demanding of faith than the indigo

light which hasn't changed, gathered high
in the dome of the tomb. Under the concrete
slab, cold as an empty bed, Lowell lies abstract.

His atoms squeezed through the vault years ago,
long before I and the angular girl I thought
I loved traded pulls from our first bottle

of cheap chianti, hiking drunk from Lovers Lane
to Mars Hill. Behind our distorted faces staring
through frosted glass at the telescope, snow

filled these woods with aspen where there had been
only scrub oak. And the color of her breath pluming
away in December was the white of a doe's

I once saw in autumn, stepping from undergrowth.
What a wreath is memory: the threadlike pencil artist
is married, has a child of five named after a boy

who wrote his mother verses once. Nine years ago,
love. Now that the town and university sprawl so
much larger than I remember them, astronomy

seems impossible. Before this hill closes to ordinary
pedestrians—the Observatory cordoned away—
think of Lowell eighty years in the past,

bent like a comma over his books,
writing of a dark gravity between stars on plates,
and unseen planets logic and desire said must be there.

for Laura

Watering the Mare
for Ken

Though she seems far away
she isn't.
She finds her distance
in unvisited corners
of the field, attended by ordinary

wrens, her blaze
a medicine rattle
moving in rabbit grass,
the elliptical
white bulb of it centering exactly

between her eyes.
They are two black beetles
watching you lead them
toward water full of their color,
the dark pond shaped

like a hand-held mirror.
After drinking she looks
strangely at you,
almost too many moments,
then blue under a rising moon

she moves away along the fence
again, seeking space, her blaze
only just visible,
a dim flame
in the direction of the river.

Garcia's Hand

Rainbow tape shifts color
on the bumper, as we shift weight,
weathered boot
to weathered boot. Pepsi,
the appaloosa mix, dances nervously
from the copper hands that work
her bridle.

How's he been —

All right, helping Garcia
down along the river
keep cattle from corn,
or up a mile landscaping
the widow's dirt drive,
barrel and century
plant where the Porsche
used to be —

Nothing much,

except this morning,

sweet-talking, lassoed the mare,
for luck ran his hand
over her blaze
and chased her loose sisters.

Caught them too, straw sail
of his hat tacking fields
green as the Dodge
we lean into now.

Sonoita Races
for Chacha

No winner yet, but I like the way
light settles that photon blanket
on your shoulders, reddens your braid.

I like your silence when I look at you
shielding your eyes with your form,
checking out the horses at the paddock—

heat pressing along the neck of my
snap-button shirt. I like that too
and the muscled quarter horses

jerking their heads against their leads
as they circle—rearing, knocking at
the sky. At the window we wager

against the odds, betting on Long Dark
Cloud, or Quiet One—leaning on
our hunches. I like my chances.

The Labor of Blossoms

Look how I come apart slowly
into my thirty-fifth year,
into a faith
crooked as rows
in the garden my daughter crosses.
See how I decay,
happy as the moth
released from her skirts
when she reaches me—

Mija, this life
isn't such a bad thing.

They say Archimedes
never pursued conclusions,
but sang in a tub every morning,
waiting to be discovered
by natural law. He understood
the sky's hard to read right—
the world
like a little girl
refuses to obey us.

So sometimes in the late afternoon,
after we make love,
my wife and I
fall silent and listen
to the airplanes
drone off into clouds. Sometimes
there's no noise
but a far siren
or a rustle of leaves, one more
apple on its voyage to earth.

Hearing out the world,
we lie in each other's arms,
or relax into lawn chairs which unravel
before the fig and peach,
drowsy each August
with the labor of blossoms.

Song

We have all the time in the world. We have no time. The bed's raft is kissing the banks of a life we recall in designs of sofa fabric, the wrinkled pattern of an art print behind glass. Because wind snaps flags over a bone orchard, the thrush alternately sits on her nest, then takes wing. We know how that feels too. Even so, the street gives up its newsgirl, her twin red braids knotted into a small tip worth more than all the petroleum fueling headlines. As your wife rises from blue sheets, and you, without shame, call the bird's three quick syllables song.

Hunter's Moon

In dawn's soft blueness a bookkeeper emerges from a dream of the Irish coast, rises to turn a diminished soap bar in the lathe of her hands. So the Hunter's Moon descends outside, light sliding through windows to coat closed ledgers, eyeglasses anchoring work brought home. Nearby the voices of birds waking to find themselves in trees. The distant sound of framers nailing interior walls. Down the hall a riddle plays out behind her son's eyes. A whirlwind of blackbirds rises in a field beyond the house, spirals around its vortex the way words do when we're looking for truth. There's a richness to this world found only in isolated moments: a monument of yellow rags by the fireplace rising into a dog chasing its tail. The spoon of pureed bananas, not yet a relic, approaching her youngest's mouth. And her own mouth opens.

The Same River Twice

Light slows
when it enters a bottle of wine.
Disappears, but
modifies the darkness there.

To drink it
is to sip a little of the sun.
To allow sunlight
to echo
around in your head
like a stray bullet in a mission bell.

Once there was a year
I drank wine
like a mountain poet,
all night watching
the river of stars
give way to a new sun.

Now, two glasses with my wife
and winter settles into my hair.

I call my children
when it's time to come in.
They complain
at leaving
jacks or hide-and-seek.
The screen door thwacks behind them.

When I latch it, I see the dead
bee in the white cup
of our rose, yellow pollen
gathered to its abdomen
like throwaway stars.

Didn't my mother show this to me
long ago on Northfield Drive,
the patched street shimmering,
a river I could stand in twice?

Wine slows life too, as we go by.
As we remember.
Words brush across my face
like wrens
who've never seen a man before.

Let Us, Like Issa, Ask Ourselves

Eminent cats, this crime spree must end.
The slain pigeon's collapsed origami
on the front porch upsets our daughter.
The whacked house finch
in his little red vest, our son.

Consider, friends, the wisdom in allowing
the tawny wrens to continue their search
through the blond grasses of summer
for whatever it is that is lost.

Otherwise,
how will you ever become Buddhas?
Let us, like Issa, ask ourselves
what law have I come to embody?

Surely, there is some dusty lesson
coded in the calligraphy of small footprints
you pause to inspect on the path this morning.

How else account for the reprimand
of this saffron veil dawn lowers,
blinding your upturned faces,
denying you knowledge
of the source of the redbird's song?

Absence

Evicted from sleep, my boy and girl
wake to absence, to memories of her
threading their legs in summer weeds.

They cobble a cross from sticks and twine,
mark the grave housing her lightness.
Puzzled, and emptied, all they want

the world back in which she tilts
her curious face, watching us prune
wild roses spilling over Saint Francis.

Redtail Hawks

Learning to be still. Learning how to listen for that icy *keen, keen*, falling through branches. Falling through new leaves where they wait in their goofy sneakers. No luck but there they are again — one more winter surrenders to spring. Up to her father's chest, the girl with the sun in her hair. The hawk's tail vanishing down the river. The beauty of the physical world's aggressive. A persistent myth. Images memory's constructed from on a depot platform where passengers wait. Trains will come for each of them. Only the times will be different. They sit patiently on plastic chairs, sipping thin coffee. Turning the pages of a daily. A man in Louisiana predicts the end of the world. The Market closes on a small rally in spite of the new regime's old bromides. If you look out the window as the train pulls away, you see the smooth roadbed stones giving up their heat. Letting the radiance go. A dark beauty entered the daughter's face when she said her name out loud to the river. Syllables splashed in the cold water. Her name sliding under the red husk of a dragonfly. The vowels brushing the legs of the spiders. Each balanced on a liquid surface where ripples broke the sun, remade the sun, then broke the sun again.

Of the Small
for Tess

Now you are grown into a lotus blossom.
That's what Po Chu-i would say
if he could see you. And he
would be speaking the truth.
He too had a daughter.
Thirteen centuries ago.
Some things remain the same
and we may count on them
to go on doing so.
When you smile I see
the hidden keys of the small
piano behind the light
rouge of your curved lips.
Today those keys put me
in mind of the song of time passing.
At my age I should know better.
How old must I be to remember —
whenever I drink this red wine
I feel like a solitary, lost
bird in the snare of flying autumn.

Big World, Little Garden

Cicadas yammer
as the sundial
throws a shadow.

The redbird that woke me
with its early song
has grown silent.

Pines hold onto
the emptiness
nesting at their centers.

In the mirror of the well,
beneath stars of yellow
blossoms, white clouds

like Taoist wanderers
find their way.
Everything important

remains unsaid.
The shadow of time
pivots slowly

along the stucco wall
joining our house
to the little garden

where suns burn
in the peach tree.
I drag the hose

over surplus ties
soaked in oil
to quench the thirst

of growing things.
Old footprints
show me where I've been,

lead me near the green
where years ago
my boy and girl

struck colored balls
with mallets, threading
wickets toward

the stake called home.
Two weeks
from yesterday

she'll be married.
Why lament
the quickness

of the wind
that leaves
the trees

alone in stillness?
Looking upward
I see birds

chase
across the sky.
She promised

there will be
grandchildren
to play with me.

Miller Canyon Trail No. 106

All morning & early afternoon clouds swell the sky
with their gray-and-white architectures,
labor toward rain. I hike alone into the mountain,

harder edges coming back in the effort of thigh
against trail—a path's shifting debris—
when I think of you, water broken, entering the tunnels

of pain which issue a son or daughter, childhood's
beatification. Often it's difficult to understand
our lives on this planet, as when we weep through bliss

at some particular sorrow's palpability: new mother
behind a curtain in the next bed, delirious, slurs
names through anesthetic for the stern-faced priest

with his gestures & sudden baptisms. I could see him,
later, from the grounds, hunched over in the rescue
helicopter as it ascended & thrashed toward Tucson.

I watched the swirl of clouds over the community hospital,
the state flags limp at their staff—navy blue & copper,
a rising sun's overconfidence. I'd like to say

I learned what makes a difference in this life
the day my boy went down into his nap & ceased
breathing—how quickly all we care about can collapse—

but it's not as easy as that. I had his sister to take home,
dinner to prepare—something simple enough for
a father to fix. I'm still unashamed for the way I

dissolved into the details of its assembly, the minutes
I wasted trying to find her favorite cartoons—
my weak gratefulness for small things. Like this year

the summer rains came late & I stayed away from my dad's
old blue Safari, its *clack, clack*, its vanity.
It doesn't make sense, but there it is: I felt my pride

could kill him. Unlike the child without a throat
or anus, my son reclaimed his life, as if he'd forgotten
something he wanted to grow up & tell us. Patty, it's crazy

how once-fierce borders grow fuzzy, merge our hands
with spoons of puffed wheat, iridescent
green shoestrings—how the loss of such ordinary tasks

can ruin us. Here, where the trail runs out
in a wood too fire-damaged to be a proper forest
of legend, I remove my shoes & set them under foliage.

I drink from my face, my lips touching the cold reflection
of my lips. What's less substantial than memory—the
dozen blue moths which break from a pool's

surface, shatter into brush & pine like a present moment?
The hand's impromptu cup of water, its ten million
invisible creatures? We want it, whatever it is.

PART III

HERE A MOMENT

Remember what you promised in July?
Never to forget the smell of horses in the barn?

— Tony Hoagland

Whitewater Draw

Twenty thousand cranes
in shallows on thin legs,
waiting for the sun.
Swamped in silence,
farmhouses,
pole barns,
ground pumps.
Globes burning over silo doors.
What's remembered
outlives itself.
The sense of deep time
one winter morning,
birds robed in sunlight,
breeze rising to open
the cornfield.
Understanding, almost.

After the Flood

The swollen river
swept away the blue heron,
the tilted gray trunks hiding her nest.

She'll rebuild,
it's easy for us to say.
Sooner or later,

the day comes when
we all do. It's easy to dismiss
the harshness of her world

if your heart doesn't beat
with that kind of intensity.
And I was expecting to see her

at watch on the log today,
her long beak pointing,
something, I don't know what,

behind the trees. Not this
hard luck
mixed with pine and mint

on the breeze, not this fawn,
sudden as rain
on my path, lifting her face,

the luminous
yellow mushroom
in her dark mouth

a sun she was swallowing.

Handmade to Last

Not all have names.
But this one does.
And a day, and a month,
and a year. The harriers
I followed
to wash up here
swoop low, hunting
the desert floor.
Blue hills behind them.
Grass rolling in breeze.
Water brown and slow
on its northern journey.
One side of the bridge,
a dog's grave with plastic
sunflowers. New cross
on the other side.
Scarlet, with green trim.
A smaller cross
cut from a tuna can
depending from
the horizontal,
throwing sunlight back
into cottonwood shadows.
Check it out.
The internet shows
over 3,000 red dots.
Each pock a death,
a piece of the rash,
the lipstick smear
of mortality
cheapening the southern
border. This cross
rooted in earth
with concrete,

handmade to last
with its curling paper
Hymn for the Migrant
anchored in stone.
With its lovely purple rosary.
Wind counting the beads.
Silence saying the prayer.

para Apolinar Rosales Mendez,
de treinta y dos años

Freight

Clipped back, the pomegranate bush seems intent,
a collection of twigs assembled to prove
some fable of unity.

Of course, the farm boy standing silent
on the vacant edge of yard
does not think this.
I think it for him while he wonders
at a slow frog disappearing
into iron depths of water.

Indecisive in the sky, the bleached
watch crystal of the sun
can do nothing but levitate.
Ash-topped ranges slump into idle granite
and slate, indifferent
to the two of us, to this setting
where we drift through fields,
unconcerned as lost mares.

Bridge timbers lurch, unheard.
Far away,
a faint whistle sounds:
freight bound from Los Angeles to El Paso . . .

I forget
what I wanted to say —
the episode of his grandfather's face —
red patch in distance
examining fence for slack,

gaze sliding over bean cans,
a plastic water jug,
and the lone white sock
which wasn't here yesterday.

First Spring, Summer Tanager

One spring, six months and some hard news later,
you get struck
by the crazy idea
Whitman is a luxury
your Existential pension can no longer support.

Down by the river, you part
the green scrim of willow to discover
the first spring tanager with orange and yellow
splatters of Abstract Expressionism
making a chaos of his face and throat

as he glows over his reflection
like a delicate, exotic lamp.
And the small desert river continues
writing its way through smooth stone and mudflats,
seeking a diction appropriate to

the undeniable acceleration of failing bodies,
or at least a consistent point of view.
Give me a break if I choose this moment
of sunlight vanishing and
reappearing in memory's repository

to admit I'm struggling to find my equilibrium,
which jumped ship somewhere
on the slow boat's voyage from October to May.
I wish that I could be as unaware of myself
as this bird I've never seen before,

centered in motion,
not understanding what motion means.
A simple metabolism gunning its engine,
idling in uncertain light,
built from the restlessness of being.

But I'm not
that pivoting face absorbing everything.
I'm staring at stones where he danced
and lifted, and I lost him to light
falling through the cosmos

of cottonwood, my vision doubling,
like a mortgage premium paid in advance,
seeing what is, and what isn't, here:
spring songbird, old friend,
May river a tune that won't come right.

for Tony Hoagland, in memoriam

Sonora

And always the wind
crosses everything:
butte, sediment, pasts—

skinny horses
in fields of stone,
auto parts rusting away.

Wind over busted axles,
leaking batteries,
the red fire that blossoms

in a mountain of recaps.
Pines trying to hold onto
their derbies of birds.

So we return
to roan ponies
without knowing why,

watching as they
eat themselves
into corners of pasture

and look up like sorry children,
as if we should lead them—
but we can't determine

if the green hummingbird
on its journey
between flowers

is more, or less
astonished than ourselves
when we step out of ourselves —

sharp scent of creosote,
radiator studded
with bees. Equivocal,

yet patient as light
coiled in grass,
ready to strike —

we hover
under hungry cirrus
in any landscape,

looking to put a roof
over some peak,
and make a house.

Relocating
To move one's body is to aim at things through it.
—Maurice Merleau-Ponty

Any future isn't pure guesswork.
When the myth wears off
any house in the next town will have gables,
will have wrens nesting.
This is how we'll talk about ourselves
odd hours on scraps of paper.

This new May I whisper *tulips*,
and the word lodges fast as color
in cups of light at the end of the garden.
I document another sun going down
and that yellow takes me back to wild roses
at the gate of the house where I lived six years,
where six winters I watched
birds weave lines
from a hole in the eave to pomegranates.

I was there yesterday,
trying to start the old car,
picking up a few things.
Wind cut a trail through pointed leaves
as if nothing had changed,
but the sparrow I saw circle
like a bruise on pond water
was gone — obsolete,
smaller than a man's remembered self.

A remembered sky is another sort of place
grounded in the partnership of words,
true and awkward as words are,
as the bluebird in Serusier's allegory
I've torn from a calendar to hang on the wall:

all wings, light as balsa—
what his two Bretons hold between them
before a gap in the hedge, the dark roofs of a far village.

Now this messenger who settles in the broken rib
of our trellis isn't blue,
but his roller-coaster flight
toward the steeple of the peeling Methodist church
is something friends can share—

a kind of handshake, or conclusion
restated by girls on skates climbing out of the park,
out of evening lush and open,
quick as an iris.

When their arms swing forward and back
sparks fly from their wheels
and the cool air fills their skirts,
the way wine between friends fills the head
and makes the house less strange;
the way names satisfy the aimed body.

Dawn Comes to a Small Farm in Southeast Arizona

Consider the wisdom of a blue crow examining bunch grass
out back where no one thinks to look. Muse on
fence line wandering off, like you, without ambition.
Let the world come in its own time, of its own will.
Red dragonflies balanced in willow, speeches birds make.
Goats bleat in the milking shed. A miller taps the bulb
above the locked door. Across the valley the yellow engines
of the freights whistle, difficult to translate. Too much work.
Consider light rising in the east beyond the baled darkness
stacked in the pole barn, beyond the galaxy ripening in
peach trees, on its way to you again this summer morning.
What's meant when they say the Universe is expanding.
Feel solar wind rushing by in the backyard where the crow
soldiers on, sticking his head into the hollow log, searching
for who-knows-what? Let it go, then, and leave it at that.

Yellow Weeds
for Deborah

An ageless man with five o'clock shadow leans his bike against a broken fence, prospecting a dumpster. So the teacher driving by remembers how she stood before a washer, hands on hips, her son emptying treasures from his pockets — arrowheads, a peacoat button's navy blue anchor. Elsewhere, time begins, measured out in proportioned counts of a cherrywood metronome. Someone's other child climbs scales, the cinnamon dachshund raising a howl at the pedals of the piano. The great composers don't notice the dust collecting on their powdered wigs. They stare out the window where a blonde girl jumps hopscotch backwards. To see her is to grow suddenly young again, flush with bottle caps. To fall under the spell of fresh-cut grass, the patience that hammers pine slats between fence posts. And the yellow weeds making their own light.

Old Sawmill Spring
for Travis

    1.

There's no doubt
those old Chinese poets
knew what they were doing,

drifting in yellow aspen,
wandering paths
of cloud shadow

with their knapsacks
of amulets, and rice.
Three miles down

from the summit,
we, too, rest at the spring,
study changing leaves.

    2.

Why not welcome age,
if it flames like topaz,
boards fire like an opal charm?

Pulling our hands from cold water,
shouting *whoa! whoa!*—
dancing away—

we become boys again.

December Fires

But who among us gives thanks?
—Han Shan

Wildfire explodes into life
up & down my neighbors' streets.
Leaves burn
their silence
into the limbs of the sleeping trees.

Each autumn we hear this poem.
We listen. But who
makes it his duty
to linger under cold tongues of flame
and become useless?
Who carves a generous
slice of absence
from his heart
to serve the domeless trees?

Han Shan,
what can anyone safely say
changes in 1300 years —
it still takes
just one leaf
to ignite
dreams of departure.

We owe it to ourselves to be foolish.
To accomplish nothing
in honor
of the quiet trees.
Our breath enough,

finally, kindled
into white flames
rising from our mouths,

licking the cold sky
in undisciplined
shapes of praise.

Plenty

A day that simple.
Nothing to be ashamed of.
I swept the porch.
I watered the willows.
I watched the cat roll in the dirt.
Clouds took their places in the sky.
I put the weeds in the bin.
Through the window saw
Maria turning the pages of a book.
Somewhere a bird sang.
No malice. No regret.
The world in my backyard
everything I need.
Everything where it belongs.
The continuity of the stars,
the changing of the moon.
The wind in the trees
here a moment, then gone.

Patterns

In the warm air under the eaves
hornets rise and fall around paper nests
like slow motion electrons
dependent on the nucleus
in a diagram of the atom
from an All About Book.

It's all beginning again: damp earth
turned for a garden, southwest wind
in the elms, the man mopping his brow
with a red handkerchief,
leaning on the old shovel.
Rusting into a sixth decade,

the American Fence Company sign
at the corner of chain link and crow.
The girl weeding irises
as her braid comes undone,
the indigo habits of the sisters
nodding under the raised blue

vein of sundown. Cosmic hustlers
dealing astonishment beyond
the reach of streetlamps —
the same constellations I copied
into my fifth-grade notebook
when the teacher wasn't looking.

Over and over I labeled
the important stars. I joined them
with my straightedge. The hunter
and the horse and the lion in a sky
of ruled lines, circling an implied
earth spinning round its sun.

GRATITUDE

Many people supported me and believed in my work over the years during which *Common Uproar* evolved. Jefferson Carter, Tony Hoagland, and David Wojahn provided friendship, advice, and suggestions which strengthened my writing and the poems in this book. I am grateful to Amy Miller, as well, for selecting my manuscript as winner of the 2019 Louis Award; and to Lana Hechtman Ayers and Tonya Namura at Concrete Wolf Press for transforming my poems into a finished collection.

My daughter, Tess, and my son, Travis, gave freely of their time and expertise to help me navigate technological issues as I prepared my manuscript for publication. Thanks also to Travis for connecting me with Tucson photographer Tony Aragon.

Deepest gratitude is due my wife, Chacha, who has believed in me and my poems, without reservation, throughout our years together. Her support has been unswerving, and sustaining.

ABOUT THE AUTHOR

Michael Bowden was born in St. Louis and grew up in Phoenix, Arizona. He holds a Bachelor of Arts degree in Philosophy from Northern Arizona University, and a Master of Fine Arts degree in Creative Writing from the University of Arizona.

In the late Seventies he founded San Pedro Press and edited *Whetstone: A Southwest Poetry Magazine*, as well as the San Pedro Pamphlet Series of Poetry. A winner of a Pushcart Prize, and the Tucson Poetry Festival Statewide contest, he's twice received Creative Writing Fellowships in Poetry from the Arizona Commission on the Arts. His poems have appeared widely in journals and anthologies.

A father of two grown children, he is retired from a 27-year teaching career. He and his wife reside in Sierra Vista, Arizona, where he spends his time hiking, conversing with birds, and daydreaming about his grandchildren.

www.ingramcontent.com/pod-product-compliance
Lightning Source LLC
Chambersburg PA
CBHW021958290426
44108CB00012B/1124